My Choice of Words
CHANGED
My Life

Rodrika Jones

I am Purposeful and I am an Encourager

BK
ROYSTON
Publishing

BK Royston Publishing
P. O. Box 4321
Jeffersonville, IN 47131
502-802-5385
http://www.bkroystonpublishing.com
bkroystonpublishing@gmail.com

Cover Design: Gad with Elite Covers
Photographer: Yero Pryor
ISBN: 978-1-951941-10-9

Printed in the United States of America

Dedication

To those who loved me and encouraged me to love
MYSELF…

To my daughters,

May the strength I found on my journey

be reflected in the love I have for you two.

Acknowledgments

First to God who lifted me when I didn't want to live and gave me purpose when all I thought I was worth was to be used by people and thrown away.

My Pretty Brown Skin Amazing, and Intelligent
First-born daughter, Dajanea

You mean the world to me; you are a major part of the sole reason I am the woman I am today. Life can be rough, and when I became a mother to you at such an early age, it became scary. **Dajanea,** you gave me hope to push through life. I wanted to give up, but you were there to encourage me with your hugs as a little girl and now with your strength as a young woman.

My Wonderful, Fine Husband, Rev. Dr. Kronski Jones

King, you stepped up and became an amazing friend to me. You took the time to get to know me and accept me with all my broken pieces. This was unheard of in my world. Your love, support, and encouragement were timeless. You showed me with the word of God how to put my own puzzle together. The way you pushed me to be great in who I was, and not what I wasn't helped shape me. Thank you, King, for being a father to our children, and allowing them both to experience every season in their lives. "You make Life Worth Living, and All of Me Loves All of You."

(P. S. I'm lost without you!)

My energetic and ambitious

Second Daughter, Rhaema Doll

Your courage and boldness give me hope and life. I love your quote, "I believe in you, believe in yourself." To be so young, you are full of life and I love every bit of it. Keep letting your light shine Rhaema.

My Mother, Ruthann

Thank you for your strength and determination. You are sometimes perceived as mean, but God has shown me it's the strength you possess that has also helped keep me. When I was a little girl, you told me, "Always **hold on,** even if it seems like you're losing, or no matter how hard they beat you down." I will never forget that, and it always comes to mind when I feel low.

My Father, Roger

Thanks for being a listening ear when I call you.

My sisters and brothers and their spouses

Tamika "Ronnie" Tasha "Marcus" Roger

"The late" Larry

and Ashley "Matthew"

You all are some real MVP's

We have always been close as brothers and sisters, but we have grown so much since Hulk passed away. I believe it's because he was taken so suddenly. It opened our eyes to know life does **not** promise us that we'll see tomorrow. Although we heard this saying a lot, it wasn't until it hit home that became a reality. Nonetheless, I thank you all for letting me be me. God is the source of my strength and you all rocked with me. Even though we don't always agree, you all still have my back. We are stronger together. We are Tiny's kids

My Mother-in-Law, Pamela

You know you are the bomb! You have been there to help me in many ways. One thing that has always stuck out is your being there to help raise our children. Although they are your grandchildren, you have gone above and beyond. Many know my children and husband are my life, so to know someone else loves them and has their interest just as much as I do is a relief. Your presence has made it possible for me to do anything for myself, including writing this book. Thank you so much.

My Father-in-law, James "Skip"

You are so loving as a bonus Father

My Best Friends Ebony and DonRicka

You two rode with me when I didn't even have a license to drive... LOL. We were like the "Blind Leading the Blind," and I love you both. Thanks for being there for me when I was bitter and didn't want to do nothing worth a second thought.

My Pastor H. Wayne and Lady Elect Kim Colbert

You two have poured so much in my life and helped shape me with the word of God through direction, correction, patience, and above all, love. I now know that I am a force to be reckoned with, and I walk in my God-given authority because of you two.

Kingdom Land Baptist Church (KLBC)

Where the spirit is embraced, love is felt, and lives are

changed!

Since my mother, Ruth, introduced me to this church in 2003, my life truly changed I truly believe it was a divine connection for me. The word was sound and relatable. I wanted what the people offered, which was love. and it was tangible. The spirit of encouragement was contagious in this church, it was a feeling I never felt before. Although I didn't even know what it was to be a Christian woman, I knew I wanted God. The whole body took me and my three-year-old daughter, Dajanea, in and loves us in the arms of Jesus.

Sister to Sister

Leslie, thanks sis for the connection. I love you and thank you for accepting me. You all are some praying sisters, and I'm so grateful to be a part. I have met many Holy Ghost spirit-filled women who want to make a difference for the kingdom. You all help to keep me grounded and remind me who I am. Martina and Rhonda, you two are lifesavers.

My New Friends

Shay and Aiesha, you ladies rock! Thanks for giving me deadlines to get this book done. I would have put it off another year just because. But you two ladies said NO and gave me till the end of June to complete it. Although I wasn't finished until the end of July, LOL, I got it done. Thank you all so much for that push and staying on me till it was done...

That's what friends are for.

Table of Contents

Good comes from a good man because of the riches he

has in his heart. Sin comes from a sinful man because of

the sin he has in his heart. The mouth speaks of what the

heart is full of.

Luke 6:45 NLV

bearing with one another, and forgiving one another, if

anyone has a complaint against another; even as Christ

forgave you, so you also *must do.*

Colossians 3:13 NKJV

They claim to know God, but by their actions, they deny

him. They are detestable, disobedient, and unfit for

doing anything good.

Titus 1:6 NIV

Don't copy the behavior and customs of this world, but

let God transform you into a new person by changing

the way you think. Then you will learn to know God's

will for you, which is good and pleasing and perfect

Romans 12:2 NLT

Set-Up

From the age of five years old, I struggled with acceptance, I tried to buy my way into people's lives by being there for every need, and by doing or being whatever, they wanted me to be. I thought this would give me a purpose in life. The word 'yes' was my answer for any and everything. I said 'yes' whether I wanted to fulfill the request or not. At age sixteen, I became a teenage mother and felt my life had turned for the worse. I went from being a broken little girl looking to people for a purpose and a reason for being alive, to a mother of a child who I had no idea how to raise. After she was born, all I wanted to do was protect and support her. I never thought I would be in a stable relationship because I didn't think I deserved it. I covered it up with hatred and bitterness for many men. But there was a man strong enough to approach me. He was patient but stern. He was consistent and wanted to love me and everything attached to me, even my daughter. Unheard of, right? Although I found a man who loved me and married me, I still was not satisfied. There was something on the inside of me that was incomplete.

Many women, like myself, move from one title to the next and never deal with the little girl inside of them. Let's deal with her and apply the word of God to bring out the woman you didn't know you could be.

Introduction

If you live by people's compliments, you'll die by their criticism!

-Steven Furtick-

Mouth and heart issues <u>Will</u> hinder you!!

Every loser has an excuse and every winner has a reason.

The moment you speak something out your mouth it will start to manifest.

SAY IT WITH ME

Your Mouth (Repeat and insert your name)

Your Work (Repeat and insert your name)

Your Fruit (Repeat and insert your name)

No matter what you've dealt with, nothing is impossible with God.

It is your time to prepare

Get Ready!

You will be motivated,

You will be empowered,

and You will be changed.

Anything worth having, is worth fighting through those negative thoughts for.

"If God be for you, He is more than the world is against you." Romans 8:31

He is more than generational curses.

He is more than a sickness.

He is more than depression.

He is more than low self-esteem.

He is more than a teenage pregnancy.

He is more than diabetes.

He is more than your failures.

He is more than your struggles.

He is more than anything that has tried to hinder you

in your life.

It's time out for playing with your potential.

Who says you can't be great?

Who says you can't be an overcomer?

Who says you can't make it?

The Devil wants you to believe your circumstances and experiences for the worse.

Yes, there is evidence the Devil possesses and uses to convince you that you will never be who God says you are. He wants you to focus on that evidence or those hopeless experiences.

Dare I say it isn't about what you can see; it's about what you can't see. What you can see is temporary, but what you can't see is eternal.

The Devil doesn't want you to believe or know who you really are. That is why he tried to break you as a child, but you must shift your mind. God was allowing you to be built. Jesus says, "For I know the plans I have for you, says the Lord, plans to prosper you and not to harm you, plans to give you a hope and a future." Jeremiah 29:11

No longer will you feel as though you must earn what has already been given to you, which are the things of God.

The Bible says in Romans 12:1, "Be ye transformed by the renewing of your mind."

Through the word of God, your transformation will come. Every dead thing will come alive. Resurrection is not an event. It is a man.

Though it were dead, yet shall it live again

You shall live again! Your heart, your joy, your mind, shall all live again! Your marriage, your relationships with your children shall live again! Your relationships with your parents shall live again! Your church membership shall live again, your ministry shall live again, and your career shall live again!

Grace is abounded to you. Even though the evidence and the proof say it's dead, Jesus will take His place in your life.

I decree and declare that your business plan will be off the ground. You will pull that book you have been writing off the shelf and finish it.

Your invention will be created because your mindset has changed. The Bible says to write the vision and make it plain.

Your marriage will thrive. Your children will be bold and confident, and they will have favor everywhere they go.

Your family will live out what God has called them to do, to be, and to become by the power of the Holy Spirit that works in us.

You will walk in your God-given authority from this moment forward.

People will no longer have a say so on what you will be in life. Experiences will not be your guide.

Know that you are fearfully and wonderfully made.

Everything God made was good and very good.

The enemy's traps will no longer work.

Your eyes will be open to his strategic plan of trying to destroy ALL you hold.

Know that our God can do exceedingly abundantly above all we could ever ask or think. The Devil cannot read your mind, and he never starts things, he only reacts. Once you speak something out of your mouth, he will run with it.

From this moment forward, you will not repeat conditional words, you will repeat truth!

Refuse to stand any longer on the outside of what God has purchased for you. God wants you to focus on your destiny and experience His promises in His word.

CHAPTER 1

What You Talking?

Speak Life

Good comes from a good man because of the

riches he has in his heart. Sin comes from a sinful

man because of the sin he has in his heart.

The mouth speaks of what the heart is full of.

Luke 6:45 NLV

"One... two... three...I can do this!" I

said. "Four...five...six whoa girl, you might

as well stop." They said, "You will never be

anything." I said, "But you can if you try."

"Seven ...eight," as my heart begins to race.

"This may be too much. Look how far you have to go." Through determination, I gain strength! I thought of all the pain I endured in life and still made it. Although the racing of my heart affected my countenance, I decided to push through and pray to God. Not long after, my thoughts changed. Doubtfully, because I was not a talker, I started with my thoughts. Romans 12:2 says, "Be ye transformed by the renewing of your mind!" My thoughts began to move from stinking thinking, that's what my Pastor H. Wayne Colbert called it. I started to see a little value in myself, and my actions soon followed in this upward direction which ultimately had a huge impact on my life. Nine...ten...eleven...twelve. "Come on, mama, you can do it." I hear my daughter saying as I look into her eyes. Even she saw me striving, I clawed my way through life, I took one step at a time and one breath at a time. As much as I strived for it not to happen, life often got the best of me. While researching, linguistics and thought processes I found it to be a struggle to comprehend what I was reading.

It seemed impossible to think about things you don't have words for, or you lack the vocabulary to express how you are truly feeling! Part of the problem was that there is more involved than just speech or thought; there is also culture. Culture involves sets of traditions, lifestyles, and habits. We pick them up from the people we grew up with, live with, and or interact with, which often shapes the way we think, which shapes the way you talk. Not to mention having that constant thought of the things spoken over our life from childhood. For me, it was, "You will never be anything, you're a whore, you're nasty, you're weak, you're just mean, you're sneaky, you will be just like every other loser." A teenage mother may think she has messed up her whole life, I sure did! Not to mention, I chose to listen to negative comments, "she thinks she's all that", "she's fake", "she has nothing to offer", and the list goes on. That's enough to make one confused, huh? "Keep going, Rodrika, you've got this," I told myself.

"Thirteen...fourteen...fifteen," I kept counting while remembering my failures in my mind, but out of my mouth, I counted my blessings. Through this self-reflected talk, I realized my life could go either way.

I had two options:

1. I could make a conscious decision to climb every day.

OR

2. I could be what people said about me while I sat and did nothing!

I decided to climb, and you can make the decision to climb too! No matter where you are at in life, you can change! God wants you to experience life and experience it abundantly but you must first, say out of your own mouth, "I'm coming out of this"! it became easier and easier the more I did it.

A mind is like a bed; you must make it up.

Everyday...be careful who you let in!!!

"As we think, we change the physical nature of our brain. We consciously direct our thinking; we can wire out toxic patterns of thinking and replace them with healthy thoughts," says Dr. Caroline Leaf in her book, *Switch on Your Brain.*

I had to become picky with my words! My husband, Kronski, taught me that I must become desperate for change. I created opportunities to make my words count and didn't waste them. The key to my success was learning to saturate my thoughts with things that made me smile. I am reminded by these words in Philippians 4:8, "Finally my, brethren, whatsoever things are true, whatsoever things are honest, whatsoever things are just, whatsoever things are pure, whatsoever things are lovely, whatsoever things are of good report; if there be any virtue, and if there be any praise, think on these things." Even when the devil tries to shift my focus to things that are not relevant to my future, and the top seems so far away, I encourage myself with positive self-talk. For example, "I have come too far to turn around." My mentor, Rev. Kim Colbert, shared that self-talk can be one of our biggest defeaters if we don't pay attention to the words we use. Learning the Word and being able to decern the voice and characteristics of God through studying, I realized I was not what people said I was. Furthermore, it is okay not to be who and what people expect. Often, it is a seed of deception to make us believe the opposite of what God says we are to get us to start to speak it. What we choose to see determines our reality. We have the power to change our reality by shifting our focus. No matter what someone has planted in us, we can uproot every plot, plan, and attack the devil has tried to speak over our lives. We were created in the image of God, full of love and grace. Consider and think about what might happen if we start to believe this? Think About It!

Learn to look to God's word for His promises for life. Say it with me, "I can be changed." All you need is faith. His Word gives hope when we feel hopeless. I kept counting, **"Sixteen,** I can do all things through Christ Jesus who strengthens me. **Seventeen,** I am fearfully and wonderfully made. **Eighteen,** Thou O Lord are a shield for me, my glory, and the lifter of my head. **Nineteen,** nothing is impossible with God.

Twenty, we belong to God, my dear children. We have already won a victory over those people because the spirit who lives in you is greater than the spirit who lives in the world.

Twenty-One "For I know the plans I have for you," declares the Lord, "plans to prosper you and not to harm you, plans to give you hope and a future." When things aren't going the way we expected, it can seem like God is against us. Becoming conscious that God is not against me, I remember God has a plan that leads to what is best for me and those around me who affect my life. It is possible to think about something even if we don't have a word for it. The Holy Spirit will intercede for us. Although we don't always know or understand God's plan for us, if we trust in Him, he will lead us to an abundant life. What we allow into our mind determines our reality and, ultimately, who we become. I consider myself a stair climber because I desire to go higher, there is no elevator to success. As the quote says, "There is no joy in living your whole life on the ground, you can't fall if you don't climb." Shift your mind. My goals were always in my view. I made a vow to climb higher than my situation looked. Count your blessings instead of counting your failures due to fear.

God Has Not Given Us the Spirit of Fear

but of Love Power and a Sound Mind!

Talking Points

When things aren't going the way we expected, it can seem like God is against us. Becoming conscious that God is not against me. Remember, God has a plan that will lead to what is best for you and those around you that affect your life. It is possible to think about something even if you don't have a word for it. The Holy Spirit will intercede for you. Although we don't always know or understand God's plan for us, if we trust in Him, He will lead us to an abundant life.

What you allow into your mind determines
your reality and, ultimately, who you
become. Good thoughts always turn things
around. Think about who is in your circle.
How have they affected you, and in what
ways?

What Type of Woman Are You?

_____
_____
_____
_____
_____
_____
_____
_____
_____
_____
_____
_____
_____
_____
_____
_____
_____
_____
_____
_____
_____
_____
_____
_____
_____
_____
_____

Reflection

_____

_____

_____

_____

_____

_____

_____

_____

_____

_____

_____

_____

_____

_____

_____

_____

_____

_____

_____

_____

_____

_____

Reflection

_____

_____

_____

_____

_____

_____

_____

_____

_____

_____

_____

_____

_____

_____

_____

_____

_____

_____

_____

_____

Chapter Two:

Forgiveness Cannot be Conditional.

"Bearing with one another, and forgiving one another, if anyone has a complaint against another; even as Christ forgave you, so you also *must do.*"

Colossians 3:13 NKJV

"How beautiful is it to stay silent when someone expects you to be enraged."

-Unknown Author

"I got it! I got it!" I said as I sang and danced. "Mama, what you got?" my daughter said, smiling. I have a fervent desire to do life well, to maximize my potential, and to reflect

the image of our Creator. 'Seriously, mama,"
my daughter said. **"I got my
DIPLOMAAAA!** Today, I have been given
a choice to pick it up too." She smiled and
clapped, "Mama, you did it." I replied, "God
did it." We got our clothes on and rode the
city bus to my high school. This was one of
the most exciting times of my life. I felt God
had truly helped me because I could see
results. Dare I say God was there all along, I
just had to trust him. I stood up tall to accept
my diploma, and I had a crowd of one
clapping for me, my baby girl. I knew that
was my first breakthrough! While others said,

I would be nothing, this day I proved them all wrong. I walked up to that counselor who didn't think I would make it and smiled as she handed me my diploma. The Bible says in Psalms 23:5, "God will prepare a table before you in the presence of your enemy." and He did just that. If I had listened, focused, and acted on what people said, I would not have graduated high school as a teenage mother.

In the flesh, I was destined to fail, but I stood tall postured and positioned to prevail. One of the definitions of posture refers to a way of dealing with or considering something; an approach or attitude. The posture or attitude we take when dealing with life and all that goes with it can impact our ability to hear from God, receive direction, and overcome difficulties. A negative attitude, hatred, and unforgiveness against others and ourselves can be the very thing that keeps us from moving forward. We are in a season, or time, where we must be in the right posture so we can be properly positioned to walk in victory. This requires us to walk by faith and not by sight. There are times when our view will have us discouraged and believing that we are far away from change when it is nearer than it appears. Do not allow what you see to shift you out of position and move backward instead of pressing forward. I once heard my sister, Martina, say, "Forgiveness is the most difficult of all spiritual practices to accomplish." Yes, it is challenging to forgive. Forgiveness is a journey, not a concept. It's not as easy to implement as, let's say, being grateful for what you have instead of what you don't have. Forgiveness must be experienced as a journey for many reasons, but primarily because we're dealing with emotions. When we experience a hurtful situation, the wall around our heart grows strong to protect us from further hurt. We don't consciously construct that wall, but our flesh will automatically create a fortress for emotional and physical survival. Perhaps your flesh thinks it's doing you a favor by creating a wall of bitterness, anger, hate, or fear, which also isolates love.

Forgiveness is a significant part of the growth and maturity in Christ. Forgiving the other person is more important for your freedom than it is for the ones that need forgiveness.

Forgiveness doesn't change the past, but it changes your future. Having my diploma was a significant accomplishment for me. I considered quitting often, because I didn't think I was going to complete it (Circumstances and experiences), but God had a plan all along!

Forgiveness can often feel like one of the hardest things you'll ever do, and sometimes it seems impossible to consider. The good news is that forgiveness is not far away. It's as simple as shifting your focus. I heard it once said, "Starve your distractions such as unforgiveness and feed your focus." Wherever the fault lies, we all can forgive and be forgiven. By forgiving, you are accepting the reality of what happened and finding ways to live in a constant state of resolution with it. You will no longer be bound to bitterness from not forgiving people. This can be a gradual process, and it doesn't necessarily have to include the person you are forgiving. Forgiveness is a choice we make. It is a decision of our will, motivated by obedience to God and his command to forgive. The Bible instructs us to forgive as the Lord forgave us, to bear with each other, and forgive whatever grievances you may have against one another.

As I stated before, after I received my

diploma, I registered for a program in cosmetology school and graduated ten months later. When I started that school the second morning in Theory class, I wrote a declaration to be closer to God when I graduated. I didn't care if I had any friends as long as I was closer to Him. Although I had always prayed to be a woman of wisdom since age thirteen, I didn't think I was capable of really becoming one. It was life's experiences that shook me up and caused me to be doubtful. I didn't even realize what I had said until my theory instructor called me out the next morning and made me read the text aloud. Later she told me the reason she called on me was that I had a goal like no one else in the class. She thought my desire to be a woman of wisdom was unusual since it had nothing to do with the cosmetology industry.

As I ponder what she said to me on that day, I believe God wanted me to hear it for myself. He wanted me to remember I was a mother who was responsible for leading so my daughter could follow and for others to watch. Forgiveness is not conditional; it is freedom.

Talking Points

Wherever the fault lies, we all can forgive and be forgiven. Forgiveness is something you do for yourself, and it can help you heal. Forgiveness doesn't change the past, but it changes your future.

The good news is that forgiveness is not far away.

A negative attitude holds hatred against others and yourself. Unforgiveness can be the very thing that keeps you from moving forward. I Stood tall Postured and Positioned to Prevail.

The posture or attitude we take when dealing with life, and all that goes with it can affect our ability to hear from God. Forgiveness is freedom.

How has unforgiveness kept you bound?

List those that you are still harboring unforgiveness for and commit the list to God! Allow him to work for you, and through you! Ask Him to release you of all ill will towards the people listed so that you can truly move to a place of peace and forgiveness!

_____
_____
_____
_____
_____
_____
_____
_____
_____
_____
_____
_____
_____
_____

Reflection

_____

_____

_____

_____

_____

_____

_____

_____

_____

_____

_____

_____

_____

_____

_____

_____

_____

_____

_____

_____

_____

Reflection

_____

_____

_____

_____

_____

_____

_____

_____

_____

_____

_____

_____

_____

_____

_____

_____

_____

_____

_____

_____

_____

_____

Reflection

Chapter 3

Intentional Direction

They claim to know God, but by their actions, they deny

Him. They are detestable, disobedient, and unfit for doing

anything good.

Titus 1:6 NKJV

Lights, camera, action! I heard it once

said, if you have no destination, any direction

will seem right. Women are pulled in so

many directions, sometimes all at the same

time. They are born a daughter, such a

precious little princess, who is cute, innocent,

and can do no wrong. A sister and best friend who you do everything with, or you are protected by her and whom you look up to. An aunt who is Made to be the "spoiler", a friend, one who tries to be the best she can be.

A girlfriend to a boy struggling to determine what he really wants from you. As we grow up, we are shaped in many ways. Our identity is not our circumstances alone. Look to God's Word for direction and correction. Only when we have the mindset to stay green enough to grow can we become all we are set out to be. Who have you looked to for guidance? Purpose? Help? Validation?

Worth? A job? An opportunity? Love? In Titus 1:6, it says, "They claim to know God, but by their actions they deny Him. They are detestable, disobedient, and unfit for doing anything good." Let's look at this scripture and apply it. As our choice of words changes our lives, so it will be with our lack of words, both of which can go either way, death or life. **Understand that being a Christian is not a place in your reach; it's a lifestyle.**

My husband and I talk about this all the time, and it's something we remind one another about quite often. Especially when my husband or I feel we each should be at a different place than we are. This is a slogan we take to heart and use to help one another stay in line with the word of God. Back to the scripture. It says, "they claim to know God." Consider what it means to know *(familiar, recognize, be aware of through observation, inquiry, or information, have developed a relationship with by spending time)*, but *(indicate the impossibility of anything other than what is being stated)* by their actions they deny *(state that one refuses to admit the truth or existence of him)*. They are detestable, disobedient, and unfit for doing anything good.

Let's think about how you claim to know God, but by your actions, you deny Him. As the word says, because we are creatures of habit, we can get stuck in doing things only because it is familiar to us, so we do it without thinking. Do you speak out of circumstances, experiences, or out of faith? Have you dealt with that little girl on the inside of you? Have a mindset to go for it and know that you can make a difference in your life. Don't be afraid to try something different and pursue opportunities that may present themselves. I have found that to be successful, our attitude must encourage openness, curiosity, and willingness to seek new challenges and opportunities. Anything that's a break from your routine is called force. The devil's goal is to sabotage your forward movement, so your brain goes into autopilot and does what it is used to doing.

Let's think about you for once.

What does a goal mean to you?

What determines your goal(s)?

How long will it take you to reach a goal?

What are your reasons for having a goal(s)?

Are the goals centered around people?

Are they someone else goals for you?

How long will it take to reach that goal?

Have you ever reached a goal that you set?

How did it feel?

What was the purpose?

These are questions I ask myself (Your Turn)

Put your life into perspective!

What does a goal mean to you?

_____

_____

_____

_____

_____

What determines your goal(s)?

_____

_____

_____

_____

_____

How long will it take you to reach a goal?

_____

_____

_____

_____

_____

What are your reasons for having a goal or goals?

_____

_____

_____

_____

_____

Are your goals centered around people?

_____

_____

_____

_____

_____

Are they someone else's goals for you?

_____

_____

_____

_____

_____

Have you ever reached a goal that you set?

_____

_____

_____

_____

_____

How did it feel?

_____

_____

_____

_____

_____

What was the purpose?

_____

_____

_____

_____

_____

In Philippians 4:6-7 it says, "Be anxious for nothing, but in everything by prayer and supplication, with thanksgiving, let your requests be made known to God; and the peace of God, which surpasses all understanding, will guard your hearts and minds through Christ Jesus."

Think About It

As you have gone through this book, building yourself up in the word of God is the common theme. Understand your mouth is a weapon, learn to stop giving unworthy things so much attention.

As long as you walk in that same circle

you will get the same results.

When you are better, everything attached to

you is better.

Know what you have and don't have to deal

with.

The power of coming in contact with who

you are in God is essential.

You are sealed and confirmed. The Word

justifies and qualifies you.

"Loneliness is a state of mind, <u>it is not</u> the

absence of people but the absence of

purpose, and when you walk in your

purpose, the right people will come along."

-Cindy Trim

"Make it up in your mind that you will no

longer be bound by people's opinions about

you.

Your identity is found in the word of God."

Your victory is sure -Pastor H. Wayne

Colbert

Reflection

_____

_____

_____

_____

_____

_____

_____

_____

_____

_____

_____

_____

_____

_____

_____

_____

_____

_____

_____

_____

_____

_____

Chapter Four:

Grin and Bear It

Don't copy the behavior and customs of this world, but let God transform you into a new person by changing the way you think. Then you will learn to know God's will for you, which is good and pleasing and perfect.

Romans 12:2 NLT

Stop! Go! Slow down! Speed up! Stop! Go! Slow down! Speed up!

"Is this that what I think it is?" I ask my husband as I was driving down the highway to take our daughter back to school. This trip was different. The whistling sound of the wind let me know it was blowing at an extremely high speed. Cars seem to be going so much faster than the speed limit considering the steady raindrops bouncing against my windshield. Then suddenly, the rain stopped. My husband said, "I am not sure what you are asking? What do you see? You are driving weird, though."

"Honestly," I responded apprehensively, "I'm not sure I know either." The trees looked like they were coming together to form a creature. Then the Holy Spirit spoke to me, "You are fearful of the unknown! Endure, Rodrika, for I am with you even until the end!" I say this same thing to you and encourage you as you read this book. Know that you can do all things through Christ Jesus who strengthens you. When we don't know what the end is going to be, naturally, we hesitate to go with the flow. As a believer, remember everything that comes into our lives is under the control of a sovereign God. He is working all things out for our good. We can turn to God with our fears and suffering; He will be faithful to help us undergo every trial and to overcome. To "endure" does not mean to simply grin and bear life as a Christian. We will feel sad, broken, unloved, confused, betrayed, or even angry at times. These emotions are not bad; they only become bad and/or even sin when we allow them to take root in our lives and produce bitterness, evil thoughts of revenge, or unforgiveness. As I have pressed through life with **resilience,** having the ability to recover from and adjust easily to misfortune and change, I have learned that divine alignment includes success! While driving on that road one rainy, windy day, what looked like a creature (the unknown) was really a healthy marriage my husband and I work towards every day, with the help of God. It was my degree in Strategic Business Communications that I am NOW studying in school. It was this book you are reading and many more to come. It was Pearl Woman, my motivational speaking and life coach company that I own. It was my certificates to start this company. It was opportunities with companies such as Commonwealth Credit Union, where I serve as a Financial Service Representative, and I can live better through financial literacy and credit building guidance. It is my affiliation with Louisville Urban League Young Professionals as an active member on the Board of the Public

Relations Committee (LUYP). While serving on this board, I created many events throughout the community. I was also allowed to write the organization's motto, which is **Support Conquer and Succeed, "Get Connected."** President and Vice-President approved. Kingdom Land Baptist Church is where I serve as the Woman's Ministry Leader. Having been led in this position, I can encourage and empower many women of all walks of life to overcome and walk in their God-given anointing. It's the many things coming that the devil doesn't want us to encounter.

I speak death to everything that stands against the knowledge and power of God. We learn to have the same joy as Paul had during trials! Find glory in our sufferings because we know "...suffering produces perseverance; perseverance, character; and character, hope." (Romans 5:3–4). Jesus is the ultimate example of someone who endured hardship, and we must endure hardship as a good soldier of Jesus Christ. (2nd Timothy 2:3) God exalts His people, and He is purpose driven. Evaluate yourself against the word of God and His holiness. From this moment forward, your conversations will line up with your vision. Deal with the little girl inside of you. Surrender to the work of the Word. Let God show you who you are, then no longer allow yourself to be bound to experiences and expectations others placed on your life. You are more than a conqueror, and you can win!

Reflection

_____
_____
_____
_____
_____
_____
_____
_____
_____
_____
_____
_____
_____
_____
_____
_____
_____
_____
_____
_____
_____

Reflection

_____

_____

_____

_____

_____

_____

_____

_____

_____

_____

_____

_____

_____

_____

_____

_____

_____

_____

_____

_____

Remember:

"You teach your mouth how to speak."

Be Motivated, Be Encouraged, and Be

Changed!

SAY IT WITH ME

I am Purposeful

Your Mouth (repeat with your name)

Your Work (repeat with your name)

Your Fruit (repeat with your name)

Talking Points

You are fearful of the unknown.

You teach your mouth to speak.

Endure, says the Lord, for I am with you

even until the end.

Know that you can do all things through

Christ Jesus who strengthens you.

As a believer, remember everything that

comes into our lives is under the control of

a sovereign God.

Turn to God with your fears and suffering.

Surrender to the work of the Word.

You are more than a conqueror, and you

can Win!

Be Motivated

Be Encouraged

Be Changed

You are purposeful

Your Choice of Words Will Change Your

Life

Reflection

Reflection

_____

_____

_____

_____

_____

_____

_____

_____

_____

_____

_____

_____

_____

_____

_____

_____

_____

_____

_____

_____

Reflection

_____

_____

_____

_____

_____

_____

_____

_____

_____

_____

_____

_____

_____

_____

_____

_____

_____

_____

_____

_____

www.ingramcontent.com/pod-product-compliance
Lightning Source LLC
Chambersburg PA
CBHW072208090426
42740CB00012B/2439